_____

Presented To

_____

Presented By

_____

Date

PROVERBS
FOR LIFE™

for Men

inspirio™

Proverbs for Life™ for Men
ISBN 0-310-80177-X

Copyright © 2003 by GRQ Ink, Inc.
Franklin, Tennessee 37067
"Proverbs for Life" is a trademark owned by GRQ, Inc.

Published by Inspirio™, The gift group of Zondervan
5300 Patterson Avenue, SE
Grand Rapids, Michigan 49530

Requests for information should be addressed to:
Inspirio™, The gift group of Zondervan
Grand Rapids, Michigan 49530
http://www.inspiriogifts.com

Compiler: Lila Empson
Associate Editor: Janice Jacobson
Project Manager: Tom Dean
Manuscript written by Richard Shahan
Design: Whisner Design Group

Ask the Lord
to bless your plans,
and you will be successful
in carrying them out.

Proverbs 16:3 gnt

Contents

Introduction

The godly wisdom in the
book of Proverbs is timeless.
Originally recorded in the days
of King Solomon, the book of Proverbs gives clear
instructions for how God expected his people to
live. By looking at modern stories, you will find
illustrations of how these proverbial principles still
relate to men today. Practical suggestions will give
you opportunities for applying these truths to your
daily life.

Proverbs for Life™ for Men can give you the kind
of direction and guidance you need to walk closer
to God and to demonstrate him to others. Enjoy
this book as you continue your spiritual journey.

*Those who are good travel a road
that avoids evil; so watch where
you are going —it may save
your life.*

— *Proverbs 16:17 GNT*

The Road of Life

The road I travel through this life
    May not be one you know.
But 'tis the path that I now tread
    My God with me shall go.
I've made some turns I wish I'd not
    Yet still my God said, "Learn
To use those times to grow inside;
    A lesson you may earn."
I want to walk in godly grace
    And with my Lord to stand.

O Lord, I need your hand.

Richard L. Shahan

Airport Delays

Ask the LORD to bless your plans, and you will be successful in carrying them out.

~ Proverbs 16:3 GNT

> I HAVE HELD
> MANY THINGS IN
> MY HANDS, AND
> I HAVE LOST
> THEM ALL; BUT
> WHATEVER I
> HAVE PLACED IN
> GOD'S HANDS,
> THAT I STILL
> POSSESS.
> —Martin Luther

After waiting in line to pass through security, Colin raced down the airline terminal. Thinking he had probably missed the final boarding call, he was shocked to find the gate area jammed with passengers. His face was tense as he approached the desk. "I have to make my connection in Atlanta. Tell me we are leaving soon?"

The attendant explained there had been mechanical problems and they were waiting on a new plane. Colin started to lose his temper. Just then he overheard another passenger remark to a business companion, "Unless you know how to repair a jet engine, it looks like we're stuck here for a while."

Colin stopped. The man was right. He certainly couldn't repair a jet engine. Why lose his temper over things he could not change? Instead, he phoned ahead, explained the situation, and rescheduled the meeting. Colin thought about this new approach. He knew he had a lot to learn.

Anyone who flies on a regular basis runs into the frustration of canceled flights, long delays, and missed connections. Similarly, many incidents happen each day that you cannot control. When that is true, accept things as they are and avoid making them worse. Taking out your frustrations on others around you serves only to demonstrate your lack of self-control. Whatever occurs, find ways to make a positive contribution to every situation. There is joy in every moment of the day when you trust God to have control.

Try this: Begin your day by asking God to guide your steps. Throughout the day, whenever you feel tense and irritated, back up and ask, Can I do anything to change this situation? If you can, do it in a positive way. If not, accept things as they are and let God fill you with his joy.

HE WHO TRUSTS
IN THE LORD
WILL PROSPER.

PROVERBS 28:25
NASB

EVERY WORD OF
GOD PROVES TRUE;
HE IS A SHIELD TO
THOSE WHO TAKE
REFUGE IN HIM.

PROVERBS 30:5
NRSV

Happiness is not the absence of conflict, but the ability to cope with i

ANONYMOUS

BEST FOOT FORWARD

Do you see a man skilled in his work? He will stand before kings; he will not stand before obscure men.

— *Proverbs 22:29* NIV

Nathan's biggest problem was himself. When he had a job to do at work, he rarely completed it on time, and his end results were often sloppy. When someone asked for his help, he was usually too busy. Nathan simply didn't work well unsupervised.

The district manager called him to set up an appointment for his annual review. At first Nathan experienced a hint of excitement. *Maybe I'll get that promotion after all.* Then he convinced himself that office politics would probably knock him out of the running.

When Nathan arrived for his review, he sat and listened as his DM went over his past year's performance. The words cut deep as Nathan learned not only was he not getting the promotion, but he was also being moved under a supervisor. Nathan realized his challenge; he needed to work harder and do a better job if he wanted to succeed.

Giving your best effort in everything you do—big or small—is important. Doing a good job is a witness to others. And by exhibiting confidence and demonstrating your strengths and abilities to those around you, you give glory to God. Reliance on and awareness of God leads you to do your job to the best of your ability even if nobody is there to notice. The way you approach a task demonstrates who you truly are on the inside.

Try this: Consider the latest assignment you received at work. Up until now, what has been your approach? What can you do to change and improve your performance? Start now giving your best effort in all you do. Recognize when you need guidance and ask for help. Take initiative, too—determine a creative new idea you can propose to your supervisor today.

YOUR REWARD DEPENDS ON WHAT YOU SAY AND WHAT YOU DO; YOU WILL GET WHAT YOU DESERVE.

PROVERBS 12:14 GNT

TRUTH, WISDOM, LEARNING AND GOOD SENSE—THESE ARE WORTH PAYING FOR, BUT TOO VALUABLE FOR YOU TO SELL.

PROVERBS 23:23 GNT

Your success depends mainly upon what you think of yourself and whether you believe in yourself.

WILLIAM J. H. BOETCKER

Hitting the Nail on the Head

A king wants to hear the truth and will favor those who speak it.

~ Proverbs 16:13 GNT

For over a year, the two men worked side by side framing houses in the new subdivision. Often they disagreed with the contractor, who constantly cut corners and purchased substandard materials. But they both kept quiet, doing what they were told because they needed their jobs.

One afternoon, the developer drove up to their job site and walked toward them. He asked them, "In all honesty, would you purchase one of these homes?" They hesitated to answer. The owner continued, "It's okay. I want to hear your opinion."

Almost in unison, the two men said no. They went on to explain the conflicts they had with the contractor. The developer listened intently, then finally responded. "Gentlemen, thank you for the truth. There are going to be some changes in the company. I hope you'll stay on with us."

Both men did stay with the company. The contractor was dismissed, and eventually both men received promotions due to their honest approach to work.

Sometimes speaking the truth may not seem like the most popular action. However, when you maintain your integrity and speak truth with kindness and gentleness, you will stand above the crowd. But honesty should never be used as an excuse to belittle or tear down a friend or colleague. Whenever possible use your words to encourage others and help them to see the freedom in living an honest life.

TRY THIS: *Pause for a moment. Did you say anything yesterday in which you may have been less than completely truthful? If so, go back to that person today and admit your mistake. Tell him or her the truth. Think before you speak, and let God guide your heart to say what is right.*

WHEN YOU TELL THE TRUTH, JUSTICE IS DONE.

PROVERBS 12:17 GNT

THE HEARTS OF WISE PEOPLE GUIDE THEIR MOUTHS. THEIR WORDS MAKE PEOPLE WANT TO LEARN MORE.

PROVERBS 16:23 NIRV

Man passes away; generations are but shadows; there is nothing stable but truth.

JOSIAH QUINCY

15

God's Leadership

The world is full of anxious care

That shows up in the face;

And wrinkles often deepen

Where a smile should take its place.

Though cares and trials weigh you down,

Your heart is tossed around.

God knows your plight, and He can make

Your life with peace abound.

William A. Bixler
and
Richard L. Shahan

Trust in the LORD with all your heart. Never rely on what you think you know. Remember the LORD in everything you do, and he will show you the right way.

— *Proverbs* 3:5–6 GNT

The fear of the LORD teaches a man wisdom, and humility comes before honor.

— *Proverbs* 15:33 NIV

Then conquer we must when our cause it is just, and this be our motto, "In God is our trust!"

Francis Scott Key

A Solid Foundation

By wisdom the LORD laid the earth's foundations, by understanding he set the heavens in place.

~ *Proverbs 3:19* NIV

The Empire State Building was built during 1930–31 in a record one year and forty-five days. It rises just over 1,453 feet from the ground with 103 floors of steel, limestone, granite, and brick weighing in excess of 365,000 tons. A total of 1,860 steps extend from the street level up to the 102nd floor.

The building does not sway. It gives, but only to a total extent of 1.48 inches in a 110-mile-per-hour wind. The architect took great pride that the building's movement off center was limited to less than 0.75 of an inch on either side.

So what holds up this mighty building and keeps it standing so tall and proud? A fifty-five-foot deep foundation of steel and concrete embedded in solid ground. A crew of 600 men working day and night dug the foundation for this engineering marvel in just forty-five days. But without these extreme footings the building would not possess its strength.

Each day, your life should be like this skyscraper: standing tall with assurance built on a solid foundation. The people around you notice how you act and react in various situations. People you don't even know form impressions of your character and integrity just through observation. When you allow God to have control of your life, your attitude and disposition will be different. The challenges of the day will not be able to knock you off your firm footings.

Try this: *Start each morning by putting God first. Then during the day when something goes wrong or you feel yourself getting frustrated, take a deep breath and remember to look at the situation from God's perspective.*

GOD HAS ALREADY PLACED JESUS CHRIST AS THE ONE AND ONLY FOUNDATION.

I CORINTHIANS 3:11 GNT

JESUS SAID, "ANYONE WHO COMES TO ME AND LISTENS TO MY WORDS AND OBEYS THEM . . . IS LIKE A MAN WHO, IN BUILDING HIS HOUSE, DUG DEEP AND LAID THE FOUNDATION ON ROCK."

LUKE 6:47–48 GNT

The greatest happiness of the greatest number is the foundation of morals and legislation.

JEREMY BENTHAM

A New Perspective

Poverty and disgrace are for the one who ignores instruction, but one who heeds reproof is honored.

~ *Proverbs 13:18 NRSV*

The doctor walked into the hospital room and sat on the side of a young man's bed. Just the day before, the patient was "the master of his own fate." He worked fourteen-hour days and ninety-hour weeks. He was climbing the ladder of success to the top. What changed over night? Crushing chest pain, numbness in his arm. Too young for a heart attack?

The doctor closed the chart and spoke calmly: "You can't keep doing it all. I want you to get a bucket of water and stick your big toe in it. When you pull it out, notice the impression you've left. That's how important you are. Today you're fine," the doctor continued. "But if you don't slow down and care for yourself physically and spiritually, the next time you won't walk out of the hospital." The doctor stood to leave and added, "Don't miss the joy in life; God has some great things in store for you."

20

꙳ Throughout life, a number of people will offer healthy doses of criticism. Some mean to be helpful, yet others only want to belittle you to make themselves feel better. Filter out the barbs and jabs that can serve only to injure your spirit. Then accept and implement what advice is given as constructive criticism. Realize that an impartial friend often has the advantage of seeing the situation from a different perspective. Maturity and success come when you can discern their intention and learn from the experiences of others.

꙳ Try this: *The next time someone offers you advice, stop to evaluate their words. Have you been trying to leave an impression in a bucket of water? Is there some insight concerning your behavior that you need to learn? Discern the wisdom of others and implement the best parts into your life. Always be open to improve.*

Listen to advice and accept instruction, and in the end you will be wise.

Proverbs 19:20 NIV

If you pay attention when you are corrected, you are wise. If you refuse to learn, you are hurting yourself. If you accept correction, you will become wiser.

Proverbs 15:31–32 GNT

A friend is someone who can see through you and still enjoys the show.

Farmer's Almanac

Ready, Willing, and Able

Take care of a fig tree and you will have figs to eat. Servants who take care of their master will be honored.

~ Proverbs 27:18 GNT

Cody was excited. It was finally the morning of the big presentation to the potential client. He had helped Andrew, his manager, for weeks. Everything was perfect. Cody had only been with the company a short time, but he had already learned a lot from Andrew.

At the office, Cody received a call from Andrew. He had taken his wife to the hospital and would not be able to be there for the presentation. He asked Cody to explain to the clients and to make the presentation for him. Cody appreciated the confidence Andrew had in him.

Cody said a prayer and walked into the meeting with the clients. He explained the situation, assuring them he had all of Andrew's material. At the completion, they signed the contract. Afterward, Cody called Andrew and shared the good news. Andrew told him how pleased and grateful he was.

❧ Whether you are at work or with a group in which you volunteer, realize that your words and actions have the potential to impact how people view the total organization. In contrast, you can also close communication with a patron through a thoughtless gesture or careless comment. You cannot overlook your involvement in the success of the group. By supporting and looking for ways to help your employer and colleagues, you will find yourself elevated to greater positions of leadership.

❧ TRY THIS: *Sit down with a pencil and a piece of paper and think about what your work is all about and what role you have in your company's success. Be specific as you list the essential duties you perform and how your efforts contribute to a quality product or service, and then resolve to do the best with your God-given ability.*

DILIGENT HANDS WILL RULE, BUT LAZINESS ENDS IN SLAVE LABOR.

PROVERBS 12:24 NIV

BEFORE DESTRUCTION ONE'S HEART IS HAUGHTY, BUT HUMILITY GOES BEFORE HONOR.

PROVERBS 18:12 NRSV

Next to doing a good job yourself the greatest joy is in having someone else do a first-class job under your direction.

WILLIAM FEATHER

Inventory Mix-Up

Honest scales and balances are from the LORD; all the weights in the bag are of his making.

~ *Proverbs* 16:11 NIV

Landon struggled to cover his overhead, pay his two employees, and have any profit left for him in his new small business. A shipment arrived from one of his suppliers. As he opened the boxes, he realized the order was doubled. Yet, the invoice only listed the original amount ordered. Landon considered it good fortune and calculated selling the extras at pure profit.

It wasn't long before he realized he couldn't do it. He would want someone to tell him if he had made such a mistake. He called the supplier, who at first didn't understand. The supplier thought he meant he had not received his full order. Finally it was clear. The supplier told him to keep the extras and an invoice would be sent the next month. When the invoice arrived, Landon was surprised to find a fifty percent discount.

People notice when you demonstrate integrity in your business practices; you don't have to say a word. The best advertisement any business can receive is word of mouth. Nevertheless, the opposite is also true—one negative experience will be told many times over. God's blessing will not be present when there is dishonesty. He requires man to strive to live by his standards of honest scales and balances. These standards will honor God and demonstrate his love to others.

Try this: As an employee, treat your employer with honesty. Do not take office supplies or equipment from work for personal use unless you pay for them—this includes such little items as pencils and paper clips. Employee discounts are not intended for friends. Use integrity in all your business dealings—God knows your heart.

If you are good, you are guided by honesty. People who can't be trusted are destroyed by their own dishonesty.

PROVERBS 11:3 GNT

The Lord hates people who use dishonest scales. He is happy with honest weights.

PROVERBS 11:1 GNT

In the time we have it is surely our duty to do all the good we can to all the people we can in all the ways we can.

WILLIAM BARCLAY

Plugged into the Power

Your path may be strewn

With flint-rocks and clod,

But He says, "Be still

And know I am God."

Our God is kind-hearted,

But you must be still

To hear His small voice

And learn of His will.

William A. Bixler

More than once I have heard God say that power belongs to him and that his love is constant.

~ *Psalm 62:11–12 GNT*

Anyone who shows respect for the LORD has a strong tower. It will be a safe place for his children.

~ *Proverbs 14:26 NIRV*

ALL POWER IS FROM THE LORD GOD, AND HAS BEEN WITH HIM ALWAYS, AND IS FROM EVERLASTING . . . FOR THE POWER OF GOD IS NEVER LOST, NOR SEVERED FROM HIM.

JOHN OF SALISBURY

Getting Through the Maze

The naïve believes everything, but the sensible man considers his steps.

~ *Proverbs 14:15 NASB*

GOD MADE THE
WORLD ROUND
SO WE COULD
NEVER BE ABLE
TO SEE TOO
FAR DOWN
THE ROAD.
—ISAK DINESEN

Harper pulled the minivan to a stop at the edge of the cornfield. "You guys all set?" The leaders of the men's group were on a weekend planning session, and the moonlight Maize Maze was their Saturday teambuilding activity. The men divided into three two-man teams to solve the six-acre labyrinth.

Dale and Mannie charged ahead, laughing, and were soon out of sight. At the first split in the path, Richard and Joe went to the right, and Mike and Harper turned to the left. But all three teams soon encountered false paths, dead ends, and trails that simply circled back. The men circled and backtracked and eventually bumped into the others at a previous starting point.

After wandering together a bit longer, they all agreed they needed help and resorted to asking the "corn cops" for directions to the exit. Even though there were various starting points, there was only one way to reach where they wanted to go.

At times, your life may feel like a maze. You may feel frustrated not knowing which way to turn. What you need to do is look up—to God. Call to him for direction. God has given you a free will; he allows you to make your own decisions each day. When you carefully consider your steps, God is able to work in your life and accomplish his plans and purposes in you. If you want a map, look no further. It is all in God's Word—the Bible.

Try this: Make a spiritual map: on plain paper, write four upcoming business or family activities (such as a family trip, a business meeting, your son's softball game). Pray, asking God to guide you through each event. Fold the map and tuck it in your Bible. Later on, say in a month or so, open it. Reflect on how God led you through those experiences.

THE ROAD THE RIGHTEOUS TRAVEL IS LIKE THE SUNRISE, GETTING BRIGHTER AND BRIGHTER UNTIL DAYLIGHT HAS COME.

PROVERBS 4:18 GNT

IN YOUR HEART YOU PLAN YOUR LIFE. BUT THE LORD DECIDES WHERE YOUR STEPS WILL TAKE YOU.

PROVERBS 16:9 NIRV

No one who accomplished things could expect to avoid mistakes. Only those who did nothing made no mistakes.

PRESIDENT HARRY S. TRUMAN

A Wise Leader

When the righteous are in authority, the people rejoice.

~ *Proverbs 29:2* NRSV

Without the assistance of the Divine Being . . . I cannot succeed. With that assistance, I cannot fail.
—Abraham Lincoln

Arriving at work early, David heard a noise from the back. Walking to the storeroom, he recognized that it was J. D., the owner of the shop, talking. David stopped and listened. J. D. was praying—specifically for David. When he finished, David asked why he had done that.

J. D. shared about a new endeavor. To be the best employers possible, he and two friends were studying some of our nation's greatest leaders. They found the secret—they were all men of prayer. George Washington at Valley Forge asked God for leadership and wisdom. Abraham Lincoln, facing a difficult national challenge, cried to God for the wisdom of Solomon to lead the people. Just as these men led people to victory, J. D. said he wanted to overcome the daily obstacles in their business.

David already respected J. D. as a great business leader. And now he knew why— J. D. was willing to yield his decisions to God's leadership.

Whether you are the president of the United States or a supervisor of a couple of employees, God can provide the wisdom and guidance you need to be successful. Being a leader is only partially dependent upon your skills and intelligence. The true character of a leader is demonstrated in his morals, his commitment to truth and fairness, and his ability to communicate direction. Ultimately, the success of a leader rests on a leader's dependence on God.

Try this: Find a godly business leader you respect. It may be someone from your workplace or someone from your church. Go to him and ask if you can become a prayer partner with him. Offer to get together once a week to share requests and pray. Learn all you can from this individual and lift him up in prayer every day.

Good people will be remembered as a blessing.

Proverbs 10:7 GNT

When the storm has swept by, the wicked are gone, but the righteous stand firm forever.

Proverbs 10:25 NIV

If you do not pray, everything can disappoint you by going wrong. If you do pray, everything can still go wrong, but not in a way that will disappoint you.

Hubert van Zeller

31

A New Kind of Kite

Intelligent people are always eager and ready to learn.

~ *Proverbs* 18:15 GNT

Grant was working in the garage when his young son asked, "Dad, what does an inventor do?" Grant began to explain that inventors create—they make things. He asked his son to think of things in their house. As the son named each item, Grant mentioned that someone had the idea and then worked to invent it. His son said, "So you mean someone invented every thing we have?" Grant agreed.

Then came the next question: "Dad, how do people know everything so they can invent?" Grant helped his son understand that inventors were not superhuman. In fact, many inventions had come about as the result of a "failure" when trying to solve a different problem. Grant also mentioned that all good inventors were continually asking questions and learning new information.

"Some inventors, son, don't even know that something is supposed to be 'impossible,' and they keep working patiently and persistently toward their God-inspired goal."

Inventors seek to change the world in which they live as they endeavor to find new approaches. Invention, however, is not just for the mechanical or intellectual geniuses. God wants every person to continue learning—to continue asking questions and dreaming new ideas. Differing viewpoints allow you to acquire insight into problems and to help generate possible solutions. Differing viewpoints allow you to incorporate the ideas of others into your efforts or to let their words spark a fresh concept within you.

Try this: Set aside ten minutes each day to think creatively. Spend the first five minutes thinking about home and the second five thinking about work. What is something you can do new or differently? Record your thoughts, research your idea or project, refine your plans, and then put them into action.

THE MIND OF ONE
WHO HAS
UNDERSTANDING
SEEKS KNOWLEDGE,
BUT THE MOUTHS
OF FOOLS FEED
ON FOLLY.

PROVERBS 15:14
NRSV

I APPLIED MY HEART
TO WHAT I
OBSERVED AND
LEARNED A LESSON
FROM WHAT I SAW.

PROVERBS 24:32 NIV

Intelligence is not something possessed once for all. It is in constant process. It's retention requires constant alertness in observing consequences, and an open-minded will to learn.

JOHN DEWEY

Some Things Never Change

Remember your former leaders,

who spoke God's message to you.

Think back on how they lived and died,

and imitate their faith.

Jesus Christ is the same yesterday,

today, and forever.

Do not let all kinds of strange teachings

lead you from the right way.

It is good to receive inner strength

from God's grace.

Hebrews 13:7–9 GNT

Listen, and I will teach you what the wise have said. Study their teachings, and you will be glad if you remember them and can quote them.

— *Proverbs* 22:17–18 GNT

Keep falsehood and lies far from me; give me neither poverty nor riches, but give me only my daily bread.

— *Proverbs* 30:8 NIV

EACH GENERATION IS A SECRET SOCIETY, AND HAS INCOMMUNICABLE ENTHUSIASMS, TASTES AND INTERESTS WHICH ARE A MYSTERY BOTH TO ITS PREDECESSORS AND TO POSTERITY.

JOHN JAY CHAPMAN

A Helping Hand

Whenever you possibly can, do good to those who need it.

— *Proverbs* 3:27 GNT

EVERYBODY IS
UNDER
OBLIGATION TO
HELP AND
SUPPORT HIS
NEIGHBOR AS
HE WOULD
HIMSELF LIKE
TO BE HELPED.
—MARTIN LUTHER

Torrential rain and hurricane force winds moved across the city during the night. The next morning, homeowners up and down the block appeared in their yards to begin assessing the damage. A few shingles were missing here and there, leaves and trash had blown everywhere, and unfortunately, a number of trees lay uprooted around the neighborhood. Yet all in all, the damage was minimal — no homes were destroyed and no lives were lost.

A large fifty-foot maple tree fell in Michael's backyard, missing the deck by just inches. Rushton, his neighbor, spoke across the fence and offered his help to clear the tree away. Michael remarked that he had a chainsaw, but he really could use the help. They worked together all afternoon stripping the branches and cutting the trunk into manageable lengths. Although Rushton had other things he could have worked on, he chose to spend time helping his neighbor. Michael was glad to know he could count on his friend.

Society has seen a sharp increase in the "cocooning effect." People consume more time within their homes and spend less time in their yards and with their neighbors. There will be times when everyone needs help. Who better to assist than those living around the person in need? Throughout the Bible are scriptures encouraging you to live a life of charity. One way you can do this is to use whatever ability and energy you have to aid those around you.

Try this: As you drive home from work some night, think of something you can do for your neighbor—perhaps mow his lawn or simply spend time talking with him. Every week, determine something you can do to encourage and demonstrate friendship to one of your neighbors.

THE RIGHTEOUS IS A GUIDE TO HIS NEIGHBOR, BUT THE WAY OF THE WICKED LEADS THEM ASTRAY.

PROVERBS 12:26
NASB

ANYONE WHO HATES HIS NEIGHBOR COMMITS SIN. BUT BLESSED IS THE PERSON WHO IS KIND TO THOSE IN NEED.

PROVERBS 14:21
NIRV

Charity is, indeed, a great thing, and a gift of God, and when it is rightly ordered likens us unto God himself, as far as that is possible; for it is charity which makes the man.

SAINT JOHN CHRYSOSTOM

Refreshing Kindness

A generous man will prosper; he who refreshes others will himself be refreshed.

— *Proverbs* 11:25 NIV

"Dad, you're almost out of gas." His young son was right. Gordon had worked late at the office, it was dark, and a heavy downpour of rain was gusting in the wind. Having already passed the gas station, his first thought was to get gas later. Then he remembered an early meeting and turned around.

After getting drenched pumping the gas, Gordon jumped back in the truck and turned the key. Nothing! What could be wrong? He got out and looked under the hood. "Need some help?" A cab driver at the next pump came over and offered to give a jump-start. They hurriedly connected the battery cables. Success! The truck was once again running as smoothly as it had been just minutes before.

Gordon said thanks and offered to pay the cabbie for his trouble. "No thanks," the cabbie said, "I'm glad to help out." The response caught him by surprise, and Gordon expressed his appreciation for the help.

You don't often think of simple kindness as being generous or refreshing—until you are on the receiving side of it. When it is unexpected and unsolicited, you realize an even greater benefit of relief to your complicated life. When you have an opportunity to do the same for someone else, you will be able to sense a true feeling of joy and self-worth because you know what kindness feels like.

Try this: The next time you notice someone in need, offer your assistance. Open the door for someone, carry her load, or bring him a cup of coffee when you get one for yourself. Make a point of spreading acts of kindness; you'll find that these acts return to you.

The righteous are like a light shining brightly; the wicked are like a lamp flickering out.

Proverbs 13:9 GNT

Wicked people bring about their own downfall by their evil deeds, but good people are protected by their integrity.

Proverbs 14:32 GNT

What value has compassion that does not take its object in its arms.

Antoine de Saint-Exupéry

39

WATER OFF A DUCK'S BACK

*If you want people to like you, forgive them when they wrong you.
Remembering wrongs can break up a friendship.*

— *Proverbs* 17:9 GNT

> A WISE MAN
> WILL MAKE
> HASTE TO
> FORGIVE,
> BECAUSE HE
> KNOWS THE TRUE
> VALUE OF TIME.
> —SAMUEL JOHNSON

Ken had just moved into a new neighborhood. The cable television was the last of the utilities to get connected. The cable company hooked up his service, but informed him that another crew would have to come out in a couple of days to bury the cable in his yard. Tired from moving and unpacking, Ken decided to relax that evening and watch television. It had been a long day and the sun was going down.

About forty minutes into the show, Ken heard a lawnmower. His next-door neighbor, was mowing his lawn — in the dark! *Oh well,* he thought, *sometimes you have to work when you can.* Suddenly the TV went black. What could possibly have happened? Then it hit him; his neighbor must have run over the cable and cut it. Ken went outside. The neighbor stood holding two ends of the cable. "I am so sorry," he said to Ken.

Right then, Ken had to choose how he would respond. He could focus on the problem, get mad and build up a grudge, and tell the other neighbors what happened. Or he could consider it poor judgment for his neighbor to cut where he couldn't see and forgive him. God's way is to let go of ill feelings when things go wrong. The choice is yours. You can dwell in the problems of the past or you can move on and enjoy the experiences of each new day.

Try this: Think about yesterday. What is one thing that really made you mad? Weigh the value of holding on to that frustration—will it change the outcome? Let that frustration roll right off of you. As you go your way through today, enjoy the scenery and the experiences. And thank God for the gift of his forgiveness.

A MAN'S DISCRETION MAKES HIM SLOW TO ANGER, AND IT IS HIS GLORY TO OVERLOOK A TRANSGRESSION.

PROVERBS 19:11
NASB

FORGIVE US THE WRONGS WE HAVE DONE, AS WE FORGIVE THE WRONGS THAT OTHERS HAVE DONE TO US.

MATTHEW 6:12
GNT

Forgiveness ought to be like a canceled note—torn in two and burned up so that it never can be shown against one.

HENRY WARD BEECHER

Recognizing the Answer

The LORD gives wisdom, and from his mouth come knowledge and understanding.

~ *Proverbs 2:6 NIV*

The story is told that as floodwater swept through a town, a man ran to the second floor of his house and prayed for God's help. His neighbor invited him to jump in a rowboat with him. The man said, "No thank you. My God will save me."

Soon the water was even higher, and the man climbed out on his roof and sat praying. Two city workers came by in a speedboat and offered to take him to a safer place. Again his reply, "I must stay. God will supply."

Before long, the floodwater loosened the house from its foundations and swept it away. The man held tight as he prayed. An emergency helicopter paused overhead and dropped a ladder. "I don't need your help. God will save me."

Unfortunately, the man drowned. When he arrived in heaven, he began to question why he had not been saved. God replied: "I sent you two boats and a helicopter. What more did you want?"

When you pray for God's intervention, know that you can't presume to know how God will choose to answer. Earnestly seek God's wisdom, and keep your mind and heart open to his rescue attempts. Avoid any preconceived notions that might block your sight of God's plan. Pray that God will bless you with understanding, and that through this understanding, you can withstand the challenges of this world.

Try this: Jot down a few dilemmas for which you asked God's help in the past. Think about how the problems or situations were resolved. Note whether the solutions were the ones you had in mind or whether they came in unanticipated forms. Use your notes as a reminder that God's lessons and his help often come in unexpected ways.

APPLY YOUR MIND TO INSTRUCTION AND YOUR EAR TO WORDS OF KNOWLEDGE.

PROVERBS 23:12
NRSV

GETTING WISDOM IS THE MOST IMPORTANT THING YOU CAN DO. WHATEVER ELSE YOU GET, GET INSIGHT.

PROVERBS 4:7 GNT

Pure wisdom always directs itself towards God; the purest wisdom is knowledge of God.

LEW WALLACE

43

One Nation Under God

Our nation's quick to celebrate,

but we should pause and think,

Our Lord's the one who brought us far,

and made our land distinct.

Let's raise the good old Stars and Stripes,

Of red and white and blue.

Let's give an honest, true salute,

And to our God be true.

William A. Bixler

and

Richard L. Shahan

A nation without God's guidance is a nation without order. Happy are those who keep God's law!

— *Proverbs* 29:18 GNT

Without the guidance of good leaders a nation falls. But many good advisers can save it.

— *Proverbs* 11:14 NIRV

WE HOLD THESE TRUTHS TO BE SELF-EVIDENT; THAT ALL MEN ARE CREATED EQUAL; THAT THEY ARE ENDOWED BY THEIR CREATOR WITH CERTAIN UNALIENABLE RIGHTS; THAT AMONG THESE ARE LIFE, LIBERTY, AND THE PURSUIT OF HAPPINESS.

THOMAS JEFFERSON

The Making of a Hero

Your reward depends on what you say and what you do; you will get what you deserve.

~ *Proverbs 12:14 GNT*

The secret of success is constancy to purpose.
—Benjamin Disraeli

Neither Moses nor David nor Paul set out to be a hero. Moses was born the son of Hebrew slaves yet was raised as a member of a royal household. David was born to a father who was a respected citizen and a mother who was known for her godliness. Paul was brought up in the best traditions of Jewish orthodoxy.

Crises challenged the life of each man. Moses sided with the Hebrews, fled the palace, heard the voice of God, and led his people to the Promised Land. David succumbed to and repented of the sins of lust and power as King of Israel, and earned God's praise as "a man after my own heart." Paul embarked on a mission to suppress the Christian church, but after being struck blind he did an about-face and became the champion of what he had tried to put down.

Each man, initially resistant, reoriented his thinking to God's will. Each became a hero.

What makes one man different from another? It is the presence of God guiding man's ability to make choices. God speaks to men through the Holy Spirit. If you listen to your conscience, you will know whether your actions are blameless or not. Following your own path causes heartache, frustration, and loneliness. The choice is yours. God is waiting to guide you and help you make the right choices.

TRY THIS: *Set aside some time tonight — at least a half-hour; a full hour if possible — to contemplate where your life has taken you. Consider challenges you've faced, detours you've had to take, unexpected breaks you've received. Can you see God's hand in these events? Now think about where you are heading and decide: Is this my direction, or is it God's?*

EVEN CHILDREN SHOW WHAT THEY ARE BY WHAT THEY DO; YOU CAN TELL IF THEY ARE HONEST AND GOOD.

PROVERBS 20:11 GNT

ONE WHO WALKS IN INTEGRITY WILL BE SAFE, BUT WHOEVER FOLLOWS CROOKED WAYS WILL FALL INTO THE PIT.

PROVERBS 28:18 NRSV

The study of God's word is the secret discipline which has formed the greatest characters.

JAMES W. ALEXANDER

Moving Day Madness

Smiling faces make you happy, and good news makes you feel better.

~ *Proverbs* 15:30 GNT

"Parker, did you hear? Kyle and AnneBlye closed on their house yesterday and are moving today. Their baby is due in about a month. AnneBlye doesn't need to be doing all that lifting. Let's go help them. I'll come by and pick you up in about five minutes."

The two men were soon on their way to their friends' apartment. They discussed how excited both of them were when they moved into their first homes. They also remembered how exhausted they had been at the end of the day because of all the work involved—and their wives hadn't been pregnant.

When they arrived at the apartment, Kyle and AnneBlye were ecstatic to see them. Even though no one had asked them to come help, the two men felt good knowing they could demonstrate their friendship by offering a helping hand. Kyle expressed his appreciation, and soon the three guys were carrying boxes and loading furniture.

A smile, a kind word, a helping hand—these are the benefits of real friendships. Each day you have the opportunity to demonstrate who you truly are on the inside by the look on your face, the words you say, and the things you do. Some guys always have something negative to say. They complain if it is raining or if the sun is shining. True friends, however, enjoy being together and find ways to encourage one another.

TRY THIS: *Look for opportunities to help a buddy. Consider when you could have used a hand—when you had to get your car to the mechanic; when you needed to get to the airport and it was too late to schedule the shuttle; when you had to load some lumber for your backyard project. Make sure your friends know that they can count on you.*

SOME FRIENDSHIPS DO NOT LAST, BUT SOME FRIENDS ARE MORE LOYAL THAN BROTHERS.

PROVERBS 18:24 GNT

HE WHO IS KIND TO THE POOR LENDS TO THE LORD, AND HE WILL REWARD HIM FOR WHAT HE HAS DONE.

PROVERBS 19:17 NIV

To have a good friend is one of the highest delights of life; to be a good friend is one of the noblest and most difficult undertakings.

ANONYMOUS

In the Dog House

He who restrains his words has knowledge, And he who has a cool spirit is a man of understanding.

~ *Proverbs 17:27 NASB*

Michael, Anton's neighbor, called first thing on Saturday morning. They talked just a few minutes before Michael politely asked, "Did you know that your dogs barked all night last night? I know your bedroom is at the other end of the house. However they were barking outside our bedroom window. Could you please do something about it?"

Oh no, thought Anton. *How many other neighbors had put up with the dogs?* He hadn't heard anything. The weather had recently turned warm. Instead of keeping the two beagles in their kennels in the garage, Anton had let them outside to sleep the previous night. Obviously, they had preferred to be in their familiar spot. Anton felt horrible—he wished Michael had called him during the night.

The two men talked calmly and worked things out. Anton apologized and assured Michael that he would make sure it didn't happen again.

Conflicts arise between neighbors, work associates, friends. It is important how you handle these crises. Your tendency could be to blow up immediately and to scream and yell. Rarely will this do anything to solve the problem; it may drive the wedge deeper and encourage retaliation. When both parties keep a calm, even-tempered attitude, you are able to resolve differences and come up with an equitable solution.

TRY THIS: *The next time you feel yourself losing your temper, stop. Count to ten in your mind, take a deep breath, lower the pitch and volume of your voice, and proceed.*

Learn to treat others the way you would want to be treated—with respect. Keep a calm spirit and speak in a peaceful manner.

HOT TEMPERS CAUSE ARGUMENTS, BUT PATIENCE BRINGS PEACE.

PROVERBS 15:18 GNT

IT IS FOOLISH TO SPEAK SCORNFULLY OF OTHERS. IF YOU ARE SMART, YOU WILL KEEP QUIET.

PROVERBS 11:12 GNT

A tart temper never mellows with age, and a sharp tongue is the only edged tool that grows keener with constant use.

WASHINGTON IRVING

Upkeep Makes a Difference

Always remember what I tell you to do.

~ Proverbs 3:1 GNT

A man too busy to take care of his health is like a mechanic too busy to take care of his tools.
—Spanish Proverb

A used-car dealer received two vehicles that were both five years old. A glance at the two cars showed him striking differences.

The first car's finish was immaculate and free of dents and scratches. The interior and trunk were vacuumed and free of stains. The car had a maintenance log showing that the oil had been changed every 3,000 miles. Annual service had never been missed. Additionally, the former owner noted that he had kept it in the garage and washed it regularly.

The dealer looked at the second car and was taken aback by its dull, dingy exterior appearance. Looking under the hood, he saw that the engine had not been maintained. When he turned the key to idle the engine, he heard the motor chug and sputter. He first thought, *How can two cars the same age be in such contrasting conditions?* But he knew. Maintenance makes an invaluable difference.

The only way to protect a car is to invest time and energy in keeping it maintained. In the same way, if you want to keep a healthy body and spirit, you must care for them daily. When you eat right and exercise, your physical well-being is preserved. When you focus on God's Word, you develop the integrity of your soul. Allow God to be your spiritual mechanic, and you will see the difference in your life.

TRY THIS: *Determine to exercise at least three times a week. Cut down on snacks, eat fruit, and drink more water. Choose a Bible verse that is meaningful to you and review it often throughout your day. Determine to spend at least ten minutes each day reading your Bible and an additional ten minutes in prayer, talking and listening to God.*

LORD, I WILL LIVE FOR YOU, FOR YOU ALONE; HEAL ME AND LET ME LIVE.

ISAIAH 38:16 GNT

OBEY THE LORD, BE HUMBLE, AND YOU WILL GET RICHES, HONOR, AND A LONG LIFE.

PROVERBS 22:4 GNT

The first test of a truly great man is his humility.

JOHN RUSKIN

Wisdom from God

The law of the Lord is perfect;

it gives new strength.

The commands of the Lord

are trustworthy,

giving wisdom to those who lack it.

The laws of the Lord are right,

and those who obey them are happy.

The commands of the Lord are just

and give understanding to the mind.

Psalm 19:7–8 GNT

My child, hold on to your wisdom and insight. Never let them get away from you.

— *Proverbs* 3:21 GNT

Do not forsake wisdom, and she will protect you; love her, and she will watch over you.

— *Proverbs* 4:6 NIV

SHOULD IT BE SAID THAT THE GREEKS DISCOVERED PHILOSOPHY BY HUMAN WISDOM. I REPLY THAT I FIND THE SCRIPTURES DECLARE ALL WISDOM TO BE A DIVINE GIFT.

SAINT CLEMENT OF ROME

Win or Lose

Truthful lips endure forever, but a lying tongue lasts only a moment.

~ *Proverbs 12:19 NIV*

"How many was that?" asked Peyton as he started to write down their golf scores. Lane told him that his was a four.

"Four?" Peyton choked, but shook his head and wrote it down. He knew it had been at least six, but it wasn't worth saying anything. They finished the last eight holes with the same manner of scorekeeping. As they entered the pro shop, they found out there was a contest for the best score on the back nine. They handed in their scorecard and went on to get a snack.

Before long they heard announced, "Congratulations to Lane Jenkins for winning today's contest. He wins a free 18-holes."

Peyton watched Lane's smile fade. Peyton wondered what was happening. Then his friend said, "I can't accept it. My stroke count wasn't accurate." Peyton was surprised that Lane owned up to it, and he admired his friend's decision.

You only fool yourself if you think others are not aware when you lie. A single lie leads to a second and a third as you continue having to cover your tracks. Often it becomes so complicated that it is impossible to remember whom you have told what and you finally end up just embarrassing yourself. It is important that you speak the truth at all times—in big things and in small. God's promise is that he will protect and provide when you remain faithful and truthful.

Try this: Listen to yourself. Do you embellish the truth? Or do you uphold godly standards? Apologize and correct yourself if you state a falsehood. Ask a family member or close friend to help you monitor, in a kind way, what you say this next week. Make a commitment to God to tell the truth in everything you say.

If you want to stay out of trouble, be careful what you say.

PROVERBS 21:23 GNT

Do not fret because of evildoers. Do not envy the wicked; for the evil have no future; the lamp of the wicked will go out.

PROVERBS 24:19–20 NRSV

Although it may not be always advisable to say all that is true, yet it is never allowable to speak against the truth.

SAINT FRANCIS DE SALES

Refreshment for the Race

Do not be wise in your own eyes; fear the LORD, and turn away from evil. It will be a healing for your flesh and a refreshment for your body.

~ *Proverbs 3:7–8 NRSV*

What is the use of running when we are not on the right road?
—German Proverb

Ask any marathon runner and he will tell you that the most important health and safety requirement is to drink plenty of fluids before, during, and after the race. It is recommended that runners drink an extra sixteen ounces of water the day before a race and then drink every twenty-five to thirty minutes during a race.

Runners are cautioned to never wait until they feel thirsty. If they wait that long, it is too late to play catch up on their water intake needs. A lack of enough water can cause a runner to have muscle cramps or even a heat stroke.

Before a race, most runners scout out the path, learn the streets and landmarks, and line out in their mind where they will grab a drink on the run. Some will even stash drink bottles along the race route. The important thing to keep in mind: If you want to stay upright, maintain the refreshment of water.

58

Just as runners must have plenty of water to survive the race, you also must be refreshed through God's Word in the daily spiritual race you are running. God is an endless source of living water. Yet it is your responsibility to seek him out and ask for his strength. If you try to run life's race on your own abilities without spiritual replenishment, you will stumble and fall. As you guard your steps, he is able help you even more.

TRY THIS: *Studies have shown that drinking eight eight-ounce glasses of water a day is basic to good health. Resolve today to start drinking your allotment. You might find it easier to drink one pint (sixteen ounces) four times a day. If you start now to drink this recommended amount of God's natural refreshment, you'll be that much closer to forming a healthy habit.*

LET YOUR EYES LOOK STRAIGHT AHEAD, FIX YOUR GAZE DIRECTLY BEFORE YOU. MAKE LEVEL PATHS FOR YOUR FEET AND TAKE ONLY WAYS THAT ARE FIRM. DO NOT SWERVE TO THE RIGHT OR THE LEFT; KEEP YOUR FOOT FROM EVIL.

PROVERBS 4:25–27
NIV

Applaud us when we run; console us when we fall; cheer us when we recover; but let us pass on —for God's sake, let us pass on!

EDMUND BURKE

Dangers of Arrogance

Pride leads to destruction, and arrogance to downfall.

~ *Proverbs 16:18 GNT*

LORD, WHERE
WE ARE WRONG,
MAKE US
WILLING TO
CHANGE; WHERE
WE ARE RIGHT,
MAKE US EASY TO
LIVE WITH.
—PETER MARSHALL

It was the week of the big game. The Lions soccer team was playing its archrival—the Knights. The Lions had had a winning season thus far, and Coach felt good going into the game. He had confidence in the team's athleticism, but lately he had begun to pick up on an arrogant attitude from the guys. He noticed they had become sloppy and were not working as hard at practice as they had at the beginning of the season. He heard several of the guys question why they needed to practice since "everyone" knew they were going to win. Coach tried to talk to the guys, but they just didn't listen; they were too busy planning their victory party.

Game day came. Some of the players showed up unprepared and late. Once again, Coach tried to talk to the guys and get them focused. Unfortunately, he couldn't help them. Their presumptuous pride got in the way, and they lost 6–0.

꧂ You may become successful in your career and capable of accomplishing great recognition and notoriety. Arrogant pride, however, will result in your downfall. When this attitude sneaks in you may become careless or demonstrate poor judgment. The strongest, most accomplished person continues learning throughout his entire lifetime. He often asks questions, acquires new skills, and weighs advice. This is a worthy goal, and the best strategy for achieving it is to keep a healthy dose of humility foremost in your life.

꧂ Try this: *Determine to learn some new skill: soccer, gardening, weight training, foreign language, surfing the Internet for Bible study Web sites, or such. Find a friend to practice with in this new venture. Having someone to be accountable to will keep you committed, and you'll be helping your friend as well. When you keep an attitude of being a novice, you maintain a healthy dose of humility.*

If you really want to gain knowledge, you must begin by having respect for the Lord. But foolish people hate wisdom and training.

PROVERBS 1:7 NIRV

Get all the advice you can, and you will succeed; without it you will fail.

PROVERBS 15:22 GNT

In humility alone lies true greatness, and that knowledge and wisdom are profitable only in so far as our lives are governed by them.

NICHOLAS OF CUSA

Pumping Mental Iron

My child, learn what I teach you

and never forget what I tell you to do.

Listen to what is wise

and try to understand it.

Yes, beg for knowledge; plead for insight.

Look for it as hard as you would

for silver or some hidden treasure.

If you do, you will know what it means

to fear the Lord and you will succeed

in learning about God.

Proverbs 2:1–5 GNT

A wise man is strong,
And a man of knowledge
increases power.

— *Proverbs* 24:5 NASB

As iron sharpens iron,
so one man sharpens
another.

— *Proverbs* 27:17 NIV

Knowledge is
the key that first
opens the hard
heart, enlarges
the affections,
and opens the
way for men
into the
kingdom of
heaven.

Jonathan Edwards

Are You Blind, Ref?

Stupid people express their anger openly, but sensible people are patient and hold it back.

~ *Proverbs* 29:11 GNT

"Are you blind, Ref? What do you mean calling a foul on me? You wouldn't know a good call if it bit you on the nose!" Devin lost his temper, and it came out in full force against the referee. Within seconds, Devin found himself red-carded by the ref and out of the game.

The next day, Devin planned to take his nephew Tyrone to his basketball game. They enjoyed practicing basketball together, and Devin taught Tyrone lots of skills to use on the court. Devin heard Tyrone tell one of his friends that he wanted to grow up to be just like his uncle.

At his nephew's game, Devin sat proudly in the stands watching. The game was tight and tensions started to rise as the final minutes neared. The ref called a foul on Tyrone. Suddenly Devin heard Tyrone yelling the same words he'd heard Devin shouting the day before—"Are you blind, Ref?"

Devin groaned. *Oh no, what have I done?*

Losing your temper and blowing up shows what little composure you possess. Every day, whether at sporting events, in the workplace, or out in the community, irritations will come your way. Maintaining calm, cool control demonstrates maturity and an ability to observe intuitively, evaluate quickly, and react appropriately. Is your example one you can be proud of? Someone is always watching and listening to you. For good or for bad, you are always teaching something.

TRY THIS: *The next time you hear yourself losing your temper, stop talking. Ask yourself what brought you to that point of frustration. If you lose your temper while playing sports, discuss it with a friend and let him sit you on the bench when he notices things getting out of hand.*

If you are patient, you can win an official over to your side. And gentle words can break a bone.

PROVERBS 25:15
NIRV

People with a hot temper do foolish things; wiser people remain calm.

PROVERBS 14:17 GNT

A torn jacket is soon mended; but hard words bruise the heart of a child.
HENRY WADSWORTH LONGFELLOW.

Bunny Slope Maneuvers

The glory of young men is their strength, and the honor of old men is their gray hair.

~ *Proverbs 20:29* NASB

A MAN'S DOUBTS
AND FEARS ARE
HIS WORST
ENEMIES.
—WILLIAM
WRIGLEY JR.

Carlos stood on his skis feeling unsteady. Concentrating hard, he told himself, *Do it right.* But no matter what the instructor said, Carlos just was not getting it.

Carlos knew there were different classes on the bunny slope, but he had not paid attention to anyone else. As he plowed towards the lodge, he was ready to give up. Suddenly a class of four- to six-year-olds came skiing across right in front of him. Looking at them, he was dumbfounded. Not only could they ski, but they also did it without poles and had a look of enjoyment on their faces.

At that moment, Carlos made the decision that if a five-year-old could do it, then he could too. Carlos began to relax and enjoy himself. The next thirty minutes of ski school were better than the entire morning had been. By afternoon, Carlos was feeling more confident and loving the experience.

The exuberance of children can teach us a lot. As adults, we often spend too much time thinking about why something won't work or worrying about the potential outcomes or safety hazards. We miss out on the joy we could be experiencing. Roger von Oech, in his book *A Whack on the Side of the Head*, wrote that play is a natural way for children to learn. He explained that they have fun because they aren't loaded down with all the supposed-to's.

Try This: *The next time you visit a park, neighborhood playground, or family gathering, observe children at play. Notice their intensity, sincerity, and fun. Resolve to infuse your life with the same childlike enthusiasm (without the childish behavior): fly a kite; ride your bike; go for a swim.*

Being cheerful keeps you healthy. It is slow death to be gloomy all the time.

Proverbs 17:22 GNT

A wise child makes a glad father, but the foolish despise their mothers.

Proverbs 15:20 NRSV

That energy which makes a child hard to manage is the energy which afterward makes him a manager of life.

Henry Ward Beecher

Okay, On the Bench!

Fools show their anger at once, but the prudent ignore an insult.

~ *Proverbs 12:16 NRSV*

Anger is one of the sinews of the soul; he that wants it hath a maimed mind.
—Thomas Fuller

Touch football was a favorite game anytime there was a family get-together. It started when they were kids, but now, even as adults, all the guys would end up out in the backyard with a football. For some of the older relatives, the game had gotten too rough. They now stood on the sidelines and cheered on the others. As the younger boys grew up, they would try to play but often lost interest and moved on to their own games after five or ten minutes.

This day was not unlike others from the past. The longer the guys played, however, the more intense the game became. Having fun was no longer important—winning the game was all that mattered. Suddenly, a fight broke out in the middle of the field. It started with verbal jabs but soon ended up with punches being thrown. How could things have gotten out of hand so quickly?

For some people, the only way to feel good about themselves is to degrade those around them. By belittling the actions or abilities of others, it makes them look better—at least in their minds. Yet truly great people have a certain sense of self-assuredness. There will always be naysayers, but you can rise above their petty jealousy and stick to your convictions. When you stay calm and composed, you defuse the attacks of those who are attempting to gain control of the situation.

RECKLESS WORDS PIERCE LIKE A SWORD, BUT THE TONGUE OF THE WISE BRINGS HEALING.

PROVERBS 12:18 NIV

Try this: The next time someone makes a derogatory remark about you, give a kind, calm response: "I know that's not true. However, you're entitled to your opinion." Maintain control of your emotions. If necessary, walk away before you say too much. You will discover that the person being rude soon disappears when there is no one to listen to him.

DON'T TAKE IT ON YOURSELF TO REPAY A WRONG. TRUST THE LORD AND HE WILL MAKE IT RIGHT.

PROVERBS 20:22 GNT

Much violence is based on the illusion that life is a property to be defended and not a gift to be shared.

HENRI NOUWEN

Sliding into Home

The name of the LORD is a strong tower; the righteous run into it and are safe.

— Proverbs 18:10 NRSV

It was the bottom of the inning in sudden-death overtime. The score was tied with no outs as the last batter took his place. There was one runner on first and another on second. The batter hit a pop-up. The pitcher caught it—one out. He instantly threw it to second—two outs. By then, the other runner had already passed third and was on his way into home.

The second baseman threw the ball with all his might toward home plate. Standing to their feet, the crowd screamed and shouted so loud the noise became deafening. Inches either way separated a total win or a total loss. As the ball began its downward arch toward the catcher, clouds of dust flew from the runner sliding into home. Silence. What was the outcome?

Finally a lone voice from the umpire. "Safe!" The crowd went wild with excitement.

᳘ Wouldn't it be great if the same intensity of excitement was generated when an individual slid into "home" with God? However, your day can get crowded with "pop-up balls," and the "screams" of those around can divert your attention. Reading and memorizing scripture as well as having fellowship with other Christian men will help you draw closer to God and will give you a response to the distractions in your life. Just as a runner will sacrifice himself to slide into home, you must make sacrifices to be at home with God.

᳘ TRY THIS: *Write down a Bible verse that encourages spending time with God on an index card and place it in an obvious place: dashboard, computer monitor, or bathroom mirror. Begin by learning one of the proverbs in this book. Repeat the verse to yourself often while taking a shower, driving to work, mowing the lawn, or working out at the gym.*

MY CHILD, DO NOT FORGET MY TEACHING, BUT LET YOUR HEART KEEP MY COMMANDMENTS.

PROVERBS 3:1 NRSV

LISTEN, MY SON, ACCEPT WHAT I SAY, AND THE YEARS OF YOUR LIFE WILL BE MANY.

PROVERBS 4:10 NIV

Everything must be decided by scripture.
CHRISTOPHER CATHERWOOD

Life's Values

What are the values

We look for today

That still will be with us

At life's closing day?

Not just what we say,

But more how we live.

These are the values

We'll prize afterwhile.

William A. Bixler

A city becomes great when the righteous give it their blessing; but a city is brought to ruin by the words of the wicked.

~ *Proverbs 11:11 GNT*

Those who aren't faithful will be paid back for what they've done. And good men will receive rewards for how they've lived.

~ *Proverbs 14:14 NIRV*

OUR FAMILIES NURTURE, PRESERVE, AND PASS ON TO EACH SUCCEEDING GENERATION THE VALUES WE SHARE AND CHERISH. . . . IN THE FAMILY WE LEARN OUR FIRST LESSONS OF GOD AND MAN, LOVE AND DISCIPLINE, RIGHTS AND RESPONSIBILITIES, HUMAN DIGNITY AND HUMAN FRAILTY.

PRESIDENT RONALD REAGAN

Commitment Takes Flight

Commit to the LORD whatever you do, and your plans will succeed.
~ *Proverbs 16:3 NIV*

Growing up in a bishop's home, Orville and Wilbur Wright were always encouraged to read, study, and pursue their interests. Their father first exposed the boys to a toy helicopter when they were ages seven and eleven. Their father motivated them to acquire all information available in order to make the most accurate decisions.

The boys were best of friends and it has been said their minds worked together to become one. Around the age of thirty, they began specifically learning about aerodynamics. In a short four and a half years, they designed and tested a manned glider, rewrote all the scientific air pressure tables, developed a wind tunnel for experimentation, and built and flew the first motorized manned flying machine—the airplane.

Their attempts at flying were ignored by many, scoffed at by most, and considered frivolous by friends. But now we can fly anywhere because two brothers were committed to each other and dedicated to the task they had resolved to accomplish.

You should have this same type of absolute resolution for the tasks God gives you. It was hard work and discouraging at times, but the Wrights never gave up. They encouraged each other on to success. Many are the skills in life that require practice, adjustment, and failure before you become proficient: walking, speaking, reading, typing, hammering, painting, and so forth. The same is true with your spiritual skills. Commit yourself to grow and become the strongest Christian you can be—God will be there to guide you to triumph.

TRY THIS: *Ask God to help you commit some upcoming project at work to the Lord. When you sense a new hill to fly over, accept the challenge and depend on him to give you guidance and wisdom to accomplish the task. Enlist the help of a fellow Christian to be a prayer partner with you and support one another.*

A MAN'S PRIDE WILL BRING HIM LOW, BUT A HUMBLE SPIRIT WILL OBTAIN HONOR.

PROVERBS 29:23
NASB

ANYONE WHO HATES WHAT HE IS TAUGHT WILL PAY FOR IT LATER. BUT A PERSON WHO RESPECTS A COMMAND WILL BE REWARDED.

PROVERBS 13:13
NIRV

Commitment means that it is possible for a man to yield the nerve center of his consent to a purpose or cause . . . more important to him than whether he lives or dies.

HOWARD THURMAN

A Well-Tuned Engine

The ways of honest people are made straight because they do what is right. But those who do what is wrong are brought down by their own sins.

~ *Proverbs* 11:5 NIRV

All the guys looked up and took noticed as an old '65 Mustang convertible rolled into the quick-lube station. An older gentleman stepped out of the car and filled out the paperwork for an oil change. The car was immaculate. The engine ran smooth; the exhaust was quiet; the interior was perfect; the exterior finish looked entirely new. The attendant asked, "Have you just restored this car?"

"No way," came the response, "I bought this car brand-new." The owner of the car described how he had struggled financially to purchase the car and then had committed to maintain the integrity of the engine. He went on to explain his routine of keeping up the lube, oil, and filter changes, as well as the spark plugs. Annually, he had the engine steam cleaned and serviced. He had taken precautions over the years to ensure long-term stability and soundness of his vehicle.

Your life is considerably more important than the engine of a car. Without proper maintenance the sludge of life will begin to clog your system. If you admit your faults and endeavor to improve, you can increase your self-esteem and value to others. You gain respect when you demonstrate integrity and consistency each day. Let others like what they see when they watch you.

Try this: At the end of each day, write a short journal of all that has happened. Ask God to help you identify areas where you need to work to improve. On the weekends, reread the past week's entries. Determine a service schedule for the next week by listing areas where you need to work to keep your life in top condition.

My son, if your heart is wise, my own heart also will be glad; and my inmost being will rejoice, when your lips speak what is right.

Proverbs 23:15–16
NASB

It is better to be patient than powerful. It is better to win control over yourself than over whole cities.

Proverbs 16:32
GNT

To rule self and subdue our passions is the more praiseworthy because so few know how to do it.

Francesco Guicciardini

The Game of Life

If you have to choose between a good reputation and great wealth, choose a good reputation.

~ *Proverbs* 22:1 GNT

Finally it was spring break. Shawn and his family had been planning for a long time to take a trip to the big theme park. As Shawn approached the ticket booth, he noticed the price breaks. Children's tickets were listed for twelve years old and under and were eighteen dollars less than the adult price.

Shawn thought for a moment. His oldest son had just turned thirteen two months ago. Who would know if he said his son was still twelve? Were they going to ask for a birth certificate? Besides, the savings would be more money that they could spend in the park for food.

The dilemma tugged at Shawn. Obviously, the right thing was to tell the truth about his son's age. But it really got to him where it hurt—in his wallet. Then Shawn considered his example to his family. He determined that he did not want his son to learn that it was okay to lie if it meant saving a few bucks.

Lying is never acceptable. God recognized that with one of the Ten Commandments. When you do it in front of your children or friends, they notice and remember. Your reputation is being developed through your own words and actions, which others observe. If you tell a lie, your child learns it is tolerable and will even begin to lie to you. People will question when they hear you lie to others whether you lie to them at times too. Your behavior displays your character and earns your reputation.

Try this: *Think with your head and not with your wallet. The amount of money you have is not as important as a reputation of truthfulness. Let your child hear you tell others the truth, even if it means costing more money at places such as the movie theater, lunch buffet, amusement park, zoo, or museum.*

THE LAMP OF THE LORD SEARCHES THE SPIRIT OF A MAN; IT SEARCHES OUT HIS INMOST BEING.

PROVERBS 20:27 NIV

THE WAY OF THE WICKED IS AN ABOMINATION TO THE LORD, BUT HE LOVES HIM WHO PURSUES RIGHTEOUSNESS.

PROVERBS 15:9 NASB

Character is what God and the angels know of us; reputation is what men and women think of us.

HORACE MANN

The Worth of Friends

With friends we have the fellowship
Of cheer and honest smiles
To help us in our daily walk
Along the toilsome miles.
We know our friends by what they do—
We read each other's eyes;
And find a wealth that's far beyond
The things that money buys.

William A. Bixler

*Friends always show
their love.*

~ *Proverbs* 17:17 GNT

*Do not forget your
friends or your father's
friends. If you are in
trouble, don't ask a
relative for help; a
nearby neighbor can help
you more than relatives
who are far away.*

~ *Proverbs* 27:10 GNT

THE GREATEST
SWEETENER OF
HUMAN LIFE IS
FRIENDSHIP. TO
RAISE THIS TO THE
HIGHEST PITCH OF
ENJOYMENT IS A
SECRET WHICH BUT
FEW DISCOVER.

JOSEPH ADDISON

†hinking Before Speaking

The more you talk, the more likely you are to sin. If you are wise, you will keep quiet.

~ *Proverbs* 10:19 GNT

Have you made the error of asking when someone's baby is due only to find out that the lady is not pregnant or that she had her baby a month ago? You usually make that mistake one time before learning to be more careful. Eric didn't seem to learn. He usually ended up sticking his foot in his mouth.

Eric struggled to lose weight. He tried diet plans and consulted with his doctor. He decided to join a fitness club to try losing weight. Talking about it at work, he made the mistake of saying: "They even have classes for new moms. You should try it, Elaine. It could really help you."

Elaine's indignant response left Eric wishing he could crawl in a hole. He couldn't believe what he had said. He knew what it was like to be overweight and to have people make comments. If only he could retrieve those words. But it was like trying to catch tadpoles in a fishnet.

Once words leave your mouth, it is impossible to take them back. It would be easier to eat soup with a fork than to retrieve your words once they are spoken. It is your responsibility to carefully monitor what you say. Avoid saying hurtful things for lack of forethought. Careless comments can separate friends and create walls of offense. Learn to speak words of encouragement and politeness. Sometimes the best thing you can do is simply be silent and listen.

TRY THIS: *Before you speak, think how people will perceive your comments. Don't always say the first thing that pops into your head. Create a new habit: when you see someone, think of something nice about him or her. These attitudes and words will come out naturally in your conversations with them and when talking to others.*

THE WORDS OF A MAN'S MOUTH ARE DEEP WATERS, BUT THE FOUNTAIN OF WISDOM IS A BUBBLING BROOK.

PROVERBS 18:4 NIV

EVEN FOOLS WHO KEEP SILENT ARE CONSIDERED WISE; WHEN THEY CLOSE THEIR LIPS, THEY ARE DEEMED INTELLIGENT.

PROVERBS 17:28 NRSV

Man does not live by words alone, despite the fact that sometimes he has to eat them.

ADLAI STEVENSON

The Rumor Mill

No one who gossips can be trusted with a secret, but you can put confidence in someone who is trustworthy.

~ *Proverbs* 11:13 GNT

WHOEVER GOSSIPS TO YOU WILL GOSSIP ABOUT YOU.
—SPANISH PROVERB

Randy and Marty were planning to take their wives to the movie. Marty suggested inviting Steve and his wife to go with them. Randy hesitated. "I don't know if that's a good idea. He's being checked for possible colon cancer tomorrow. His wife told my wife that he just doesn't want to have to discuss it with everyone."

Marty looked puzzled and asked, "Are you sure you heard right? We were over at their house this weekend, and he didn't say anything to me. Maybe I should give him a call and find out what's going on."

Randy quickly remarked: "Just be sure you don't mention that I'm the one who told you. I wouldn't want him to think I can't keep a secret. And be sure to tell me what you find out. I need to let Jonathan know too."

Marty made a mental note not to tell Randy or his wife anything he wanted to be kept secret.

Just as others do, there are times when you have details about your life you want kept private. You may seek out a trusted friend in whom you can confide and who can help you think through the issues. You never expect him to betray you. Some people love to gather information and then go around spreading their "knowledge" to everyone they know. Learn to be a genuine friend by protecting the secrets that have been shared with you.

Try this: The next time someone tells you something that is confidential, pray for that person but keep it between yourself and God. Encourage your friend to address his issues honestly and directly, but let him decide who should know the details. Refuse to talk about it to other people. Instead, be known as a trustworthy friend.

A GOSSIP CAN NEVER KEEP A SECRET. STAY AWAY FROM PEOPLE WHO TALK TOO MUCH.

PROVERBS 20:19 GNT

A PERVERSE MAN STIRS UP DISSENSION, AND A GOSSIP SEPARATES CLOSE FRIENDS.

PROVERBS 16:28 NIV

Never tell evil of a man if you do not know it for a certainty; and if you do know it for a certainty, then ask yourself, "Why should I tell it?"

JOHANN KASPAR LAVATER

Speaking Gentle Words

A gentle answer quiets anger, but a harsh one stirs it up.

~ *Proverbs 15:1 GNT*

GOD TAKES
LIFE'S BROKEN
PIECES AND
GIVES US
UNBROKEN
PEACE.
—WILBERT
DONALD GOUGH

Wayne stood talking with several guys about the neighborhood entrance. Don was critical of the way the flowers and shrubs had been planted. He complained about the colors and the shrub sizes. Wayne spoke, "It's early in the season. I think the shrubbery will grow nicely."

Don retorted, "Why do you care so much? I think we should vote on what gets planted out there."

Wayne simply said, "You're right; there really is a lot to consider," and walked away.

Karl turned to Don and said, "Wayne works for a nursery. He got the plants donated and then had a buddy from work help install them."

Shortly, Don knocked on Wayne's door. Don wanted to apologize: "Hey, man, I had no idea. I'm sorry. The plants look good—I shouldn't criticize if I'm not willing to be a part of the process. I appreciate what you've done. Let me know next time and I'll help you."

꙰ Nearly every day, someone will say something that will be offensive to you. The way you respond to these situations reflects your ability to follow scriptural advice. When an individual is upset or unwilling to hear another viewpoint, you waste your time and risk escalating the situation to an argumentative level to argue. The best way to respond is with simple, peaceful words. At times, it's even best to not say anything or simply to walk away. Speaking gentle words takes away anger and allows the situation to remain in control.

꙰ TRY THIS: *The next time someone says something that offends you, avoid a knee-jerk reply. Collect yourself and then respond with a few short, positive words in a calm voice. If you feel yourself getting angry and on the verge of lashing out, excuse yourself from the situation before you say the wrong thing.*

BE CAREFUL WHAT YOU SAY AND PROTECT YOUR LIFE. A CARELESS TALKER DESTROYS HIMSELF.

PROVERBS 13:3 GNT

THE HEART OF THE RIGHTEOUS PONDERS HOW TO ANSWER, BUT THE MOUTH OF THE WICKED POURS OUT EVIL THINGS.

PROVERBS 15:28 NASB

Peace . . . involves mutual respect and confidence between peoples and nations. Like a cathedral, peace must be constructed patiently and with unshakable faith.

POPE JOHN PAUL II

Family Heritage

Dear Lord,

help me a man of faith to be

just like the man

who taught his faith to me.

The one who always gave his all to you

And always to your precious words

stayed true.

The one who stood before me all his days

And showed me how to walk

in heaven's ways.

Garrett Rodgers

Son, do what your father tells you and never forget what your mother taught you. . . . Their instructions are a shining light; their correction can teach you how to live.

~ *Proverbs 6:20, 23 GNT*

Wise children make their fathers proud of them.

~ *Proverbs 10:1 GNT*

The Christian home is the Master's workshop where the process of character-molding is silently, lovingly, faithfully and successfully carried on.

Richard Monckton Milnes

Mirror, Mirror on the Wall

It is your own face that you see reflected in the water and it is your own self that you see in your heart.

~ *Proverbs* 27:19 GNT

Dylan stood in front of the mirror shaving, the same way he did every morning. But this morning something was different. What he saw made him stop and look at himself more intently. Who was that man looking back at him? His face looked more like his father's than he'd ever noticed before.

Today was a milestone birthday for Dylan—his fortieth. He was excited, but he was also contemplative. What had he done with his life thus far? What more did he want to accomplish? When he was young, he'd had big plans for his life. Now his values had changed. Material stuff was not nearly so important as it used to be.

As he stared back in the mirror, he wondered if he was becoming his father or if he was just growing up. Either way, he liked the person he saw, and he looked forward to many more years.

Nothing splendid has ever been achieved except by those who dared believe that something inside them was superior to circumstances.
—Bruce Barton

90

The person you are on the inside is someone only you truly know. However, the attitudes and values in your heart are expressed each day on your face, in your voice, and through your actions. While outside circumstances do influence you, who you are is clearly demonstrated in the way you handle everyday situations. Others can see when God is living on the inside of your heart. His Spirit gives you peace and joy even in challenging situations.

TRY THIS: *Birthdays happen with rigid regularity. Use them as an opportunity to reflect on your past year. Write goals for the next year: what you will do for yourself, what you will do to help others, and how you will grow closer to God. Tuck them inside one of your birthday cards and store in your sock drawer until next year.*

A HAPPY HEART MAKES THE FACE CHEERFUL, BUT HEARTACHE CRUSHES THE SPIRIT.

PROVERBS 15:13 NIV

THE WISE IN HEART WILL BE CALLED DISCERNING, AND SWEETNESS OF SPEECH INCREASES PERSUASIVENESS.

PROVERBS 16:21 NASB

He that respects himself is safe from others; he wears a coat of mail that none can pierce.

HENRY W. LONGFELLOW

It Was Only a Box Knife

Teach children how they should live, and they will remember it all their life.

~ *Proverbs* 22:6 GNT

Four-year-old Isaac and his dad, Tom, stopped by the grocery store for a couple of items. At home, when Isaac went off to play, his dad noticed something in his hands. It was a small gray box knife, no doubt left by a grocery stock boy. "Where did you get that?" asked Tom.

"I found it," Isaac replied.

Upon further questioning Tom learned that Isaac found it on the floor at the grocery store, picked it up, and brought it home in his pocket. Tom thought this was a careless mistake by a stock boy that could have injured Isaac, and Isaac took something that didn't belong to him—he had stolen something.

Tom explained to Isaac why it was wrong to keep the box knife as they drove back to the store. At first Isaac was reluctant, but finally he gave it back and apologized. Tom helped Isaac learn a lifelong lesson.

꩜ In their everyday experiences—such as finding a box knife, apologizing, and returning it—children develop habits and attitudes that will last a lifetime. It is your responsibility as a parent to teach them the right thing to do at all times. The best way to teach this is by your own example, but you also guide them through positive constructive discipline. When you see your children doing wrong, you need to correct them and teach them how to make it right.

꩜ TRY THIS: *Be mindful of everything your children (or nieces or nephews) do. Don't excuse their actions just because they are young. Guide them to correct their actions. Teach them the right thing to do in a variety of circumstances. Be an example of godly conduct through your own behavior. Let them hear and see your honesty.*

EVEN A CHILD IS KNOWN BY HIS ACTIONS, BY WHETHER HIS CONDUCT IS PURE AND RIGHT.

PROVERBS 20:11 NIV

IF A CHILD IS CORRECTED, HE BECOMES WISE. BUT A CHILD LEFT TO HIMSELF BRINGS SHAME TO HIS MOTHER.

PROVERBS 29:15 NIRV

All profitable correction comes from a calm, peaceful mind.
SAINT FRANCIS DE SALES

In the Living Years

My son, listen to your father's advice.

~ *Proverbs 1:8 NIRV*

EVERY NOBLE YOUTH LOOKS BACK, AS TO THE CHIEFEST JOY WHICH THIS WORLD'S HONOR EVER GAVE HIM, TO THE MOMENT WHEN FIRST HE SAW HIS FATHER'S EYES FLASH WITH PRIDE.

—JOHN RUSKIN

Consider this popular satirical outline on how a father matures, at least as perceived by his child:

4 years: My daddy can do anything.

7 years: My dad knows a whole lot.

9 years: Dad doesn't know quite everything.

12 years: Dad just doesn't understand

16 years: Dad is old-fashioned

21 years: That man is out of touch.

25 years: Dad's okay.

30 years: I wonder what Dad thinks about this?

50 years: What would Dad have thought about that?

60 years: I wish I could talk it over with Dad once more.

Does dear old Dad actually change from super intelligent to totally ignorant to trusted adviser? Not at all. Rather, perceptions change. This same progression has been noted for years. Typically, it is when you yourself become a father that you begin to understand your own father. Are you now at the point where you can relate to this?

Fathers are certainly not perfect. In fact, all fathers make mistakes along the way. Make God, your heavenly Father, your role model. He will teach you how to mold and shape your way of thinking. He will help you alter your behavior as you follow his example. Earthly fathers have years of experience and insight that they, too, can share. The benefits of fatherly advice often go unmeasured until it's too late to express appreciation. Grasp the opportunities that are yours today.

A wise son heeds his father's instruction, but a mocker does not listen to rebuke.

Proverbs 13:1 NIV

Try this: *Don't wait. If your father is alive, telephone him, write him, or take him to lunch and tell him how much you have appreciated his past wisdom and counsel. Recall special memories and advice he gave you when you were younger. Take advantage of learning all you can during his living years.*

Listen to your father; without him you would not exist.

Proverbs 23:22 GNT

What a father says to his children is not heard by the world, but it will be heard by posterity.

Jean Paul Richter

What's Really Important?

Your money can be gone in a flash, as if it had grown wings and flown away like an eagle.

— *Proverbs* 23:5 GNT

WEALTH DESIRED FOR ITS OWN SAKE OBSTRUCTS THE INCREASE OF VIRTUE, AND LARGE POSSESSIONS IN THE HANDS OF SELFISH MEN HAVE A BAD TENDENCY.
—JOHN WOOLMAN

Leon had dreamed of owning a roadster—DOHC sixteen-valve engine, short-throw shifter with rack-and-pinion steering, and four-wheel double-wishbone suspension. He had saved his money for the past few years so he could pay cash, and the dealership had special-ordered his roadster in cherry red. The car was classic, it was smooth cruising, it was perfect.

On a Saturday, Leon drove his sporty convertible to the mall, but when he walked out to the parking lot, he was stunned to see an eight-inch dent in the driver-side door. His thoughts churned. *What irresponsible jerk did this?* He hadn't even had the car a month.

Leon fumed as he drove home. He unloaded on his wife, Dixie, who listened for an hour before Leon calmed down. It took awhile, but Leon realized that he was treasuring the car too much. Finally Leon could say that it was just a car, and, besides that, the dent could be fixed and he had ample insurance.

People sometimes have a tendency to get caught up with material things—it may be a car, a house, a golf club, a painting, a camera, or a DVD player. But all these are just "things." They all will wear out. They are not eternal. It's not bad to have these; it only becomes a problem when you focus on your things and miss out on what is really important. Money and things are but temporary. What will last forever is your relationship with God.

Try this: *Evaluate how much time and energy you are putting into temporal things. Are you putting that same amount of time into your relationship with God? Each day, take ten to fifteen minutes in the morning or at night to read one chapter from the book of Psalms. Then spend the rest of the time in prayer.*

Better to be poor and fear the Lord than to be rich and in trouble.

Proverbs 15:16 GNT

Do not weary yourself to gain wealth, cease from your consideration of it.

Proverbs 23:4 NASB

Faith is often strengthened right at the place of disappointment.

Rodney McBride

Now Is the Time

If we can see some good in man
Let's not withhold our praise.
It may be just the thing he needs
To brighten up his days;
A word of true encouragement,
A kind and honest smile,
A hearty handshake are the things
That make a life worthwhile.

William. A. Bixler
and
Richard L. Shahan

Kind words are like honey—sweet to the taste and good for your health.

~ *Proverbs 16:24 GNT*

A word aptly spoken is like apples of gold in settings of silver.

~ *Proverbs 25:11 NIV*

ALL THE KINDNESS
WHICH A MAN
PUTS OUT INTO THE
WORLD WORKS ON
THE HEART AND
THOUGHTS OF
MANKIND.

ALBERT SCHWEITZER

The Clock's Ticking

Those who don't correct their children hate them. But those who love them are careful to train them.

~ *Proverbs* 13:24 NIRV

Alan watched as Jonathan, one of his three-year-old twins, built an elaborate road system with his blocks. David, Jonathan's brother, suddenly stormed through the room, kicking blocks in all directions. Alan stopped him and looked him straight in the eyes. He calmly reminded David of one of their rules: you only knock apart blocks that you have built, not what someone else has built.

Alan placed a small chair to one side of the room and told David he would have to sit in time-out for three minutes. David struggled as he sat and had to watch Jonathan get to continue playing. At the end of the three minutes, Alan asked David to tell him why he had to sit in time out. Then he asked his son to tell him what he was going to do differently next time.

An important aspect of parenting is knowing how to lovingly and positively discipline your child. The goal as a parent is to raise a child who will eventually discipline himself or herself as an adult—self-discipline. It is essential to teach your child to think through his actions and to correct them. A child allowed to constantly repeat misbehavior will soon be immune to correcting by parents and other social authorities. Children need and want discipline. It is your responsibility to be that positive guide in their lives.

Try this: *Use positive discipline with your children from an early age. Let them experience the consequences for their actions. Teach them the right words and behavior for the next time. You may have to stay with young children in time-out, but soon they will be able to sit on their own. Being consistent has the best long-term affect.*

> Discipline your children while they are young enough to learn. If you don't, you are helping them destroy themselves.
>
> PROVERBS 19:18 GNT

> Discipline your children and you can always be proud of them. They will never give you reason to be ashamed.
>
> PROVERBS 29:17 GNT

We must first be made good before we can do good; we must first be made just before our works can please God.

HUGH LATIMER

Title of Honor

Grandparents are proud of their grandchildren, just as children are proud of their parents

~ *Proverbs* 17:6 GNT

CHILDREN HAVE NEVER BEEN VERY GOOD AT LISTENING TO THEIR ELDERS, BUT THEY HAVE NEVER FAILED TO IMITATE THEM.
—JAMES BALDWIN

Andre beamed as he heard his five-year-old son talking to the boy next door: "My dad is the greatest in the world. He can do anything. He's better than Batman or Spider-Man. Mom said Daddy flew home from work yesterday!"

Oops, maybe his son misunderstood a bit. It was a fast trip, but it was in the car. Nevertheless, Andre took his son's words to heart. He realized the impact he was having on him. Andre reflected on the things he had done over the past week, the places he had been, and the words he had said. Was this the kind of man he wanted his son to become?

Andre made a commitment right then to be more of a godly role model for his son. With God's help, he would work on eliminating his bad habits and any negative conversation. Andre called out to his son: "Hey, Buddy, let's go for a ride. I want to show you my favorite way to 'fly.'"

꒰ Children are always learning—the good and the bad. They are watching you and learning something. When you are speeding, you don't have to say a word; they know. When you are rude to a waitress, they hear it and learn the attitude. Every day, in hundreds of small words and gestures, your children observe the most influential role model of their life. Do you like the person your son or daughter is becoming? Consider your example and determine if there are behaviors you need to change.

꒰ TRY THIS: *Plan a special night out for just you and your child. Go to a favorite place to eat. Spend time talking to each other—listen more than you talk. Learn what things make your child happy or scared; find out who is his or her hero. Then do something fun together, like miniature golf, skating, or tag in the park.*

CHILDREN ARE FORTUNATE IF THEY HAVE A FATHER WHO IS HONEST AND DOES WHAT IS RIGHT.

PROVERBS 20:7 GNT

THE GOOD MAN'S CHILDREN WILL BE POWERFUL IN THE LAND; HIS DESCENDANTS WILL BE BLESSED.

PSALM 112:2 GNT

Each child is an adventure into a better life—an opportunity to change the old pattern and make it new.

HUBERT H. HUMPHREY

More Precious than Jewels

Be faithful to your own wife and give your love to her alone.

~ *Proverbs* 5:15 GNT

The wedding ceremony had started. Karl stood looking out at all the friends who were sitting there. His mind raced in different directions. *I love Jennifer so much,* he thought. *Will I be able to support her? How am I going to make the transition from being single to being married? I want to be the best husband to Jennifer that I possibly can.*

Then the fanfare began, the doors opened, and in walked Jennifer—the most beautiful woman in his life. Suddenly Karl felt any self-doubt in his heart disappear. He and Jennifer had spent many hours talking and praying about their future. He knew God had brought them together and their future was in his hands. Karl remembered the words his pastor had shared: "You can't see beyond today, but God can. Put him first in your marriage and he will guide you."

Marriage is a lifelong commitment. It is not something to rush into, and yet it can't be completely mapped out. Before you marry, seek God's guidance to make the right choice. Then accept your responsibility to provide, protect, and encourage. Treasure the wife God gives you as "more precious than jewels." Always uphold your commitment before God to place her needs above your own. Marriage is a work in progress—each day brings new challenges and joys. Put your faith in God and give him first place in your marriage.

Try This: If you are married, write a list of ten things that you love about your wife. Then make a list of five things you can do to encourage and support her. Pray through these lists, thanking God for your lovely wife and committing to treasure her always.

How hard it is to find a capable wife! She is worth far more than jewels! Her husband puts his confidence in her, and he will never be poor.

PROVERBS 31:10–11
GNT

Find a wife and you find a good thing; it shows that the LORD is good to you.

PROVERBS 18:22
GNT

There is no joy, no comfort, no sweetness, no pleasure in the world like to that of a good wife.

ROBERT BURTON

THE GOOD LIFE

Oh make us now within our hearts

A neighbor and a friend

To every man on every day

Unto the very end.

We need to make each moment count

To help some one take heart,

Then this will be a better world

Because we've done our part.

William A. Bixler

Obey the LORD and you will live a long life, content and safe from harm.

— *Proverbs 19:23* GNT

Keep God's laws and you will live longer; if you ignore them, you will die.

— *Proverbs 19:16* GNT

GOD HATH GIVEN TO MAN A SHORT TIME HERE UPON EARTH, AND YET UPON THIS SHORT TIME ETERNITY DEPENDS.

JEREMY TAYLOR

Learning to Honk

If you trick an honest person into doing evil, you will fall into your own trap. The innocent will be well rewarded.

~ *Proverbs* 28:10 GNT

If you want to change people without giving offense or arousing resentment, use encouragement.
—Dale Carnegie

A characteristic V formation of geese was flying overhead as Trey asked Miguel how to be a good leader. Miguel pointed upward and stated, "Follow the geese." He went on to explain that as geese flap their wings, they create an uplift for the birds behind. The V shape gives the flock an added seventy-one percent greater flying range than for any bird flying alone. They work together as a team.

But the V formation is for more than just lift. The head goose encounters the greatest wind resistance. When he tires, he rotates to the far back position where he can rest. The next goose moves forward, taking the lead position. The geese on the sides constantly honk, encouraging the leader to keep up his speed.

Miguel said, "If you want to be a good leader, take turns with the hard tasks. Learn to allow those you work with to be successful. Encourage them. The best leader makes those around him look good too."

Whether at home, work, church, or in civic groups, you have many opportunities to share common direction and purpose with people. Just as with the geese, it is quicker and easier when everyone proceeds in the same direction, uniting the thrust of one another. Sharing leadership responsibilities allows you to utilize your strengths and to find times of rest. You can be a cheering section by "honking" to those around you, encouraging them to continue in their good efforts.

Try this: *Make a deliberate effort to say something kind and encouraging to every person you work with today. It only has to be a simple comment in passing — "Nice shirt," "Good job," or "Great plan." Do your own informal, mini-survey. Pay attention to whether your "honking" encouraged others on your team toward success.*

A tongue that brings healing is like a tree of life. But a tongue that tells lies produces a broken spirit.

PROVERBS 15:4 NIRV

The mouth of the righteous is a fountain of life, but the mouth of the wicked conceals violence.

PROVERBS 10:11 NRSV

All we can ever do in the way of good to people is to encourage them to do good to themselves.

RANDOLPH BOURNE

Do It Now

Plan carefully what you do, and whatever you do will turn out right.

~ *Proverbs 4:26* GNT

Nick had been out of work for three weeks. He had known the downsize was coming, but he hadn't expected to be caught in it. *What's wrong with me?* Nick thought. He rationalized that he needed to get his résumé updated before he started looking for a new job, but he knew that was just an excuse. He just couldn't make himself get started.

Each morning he'd vow anew to check out leads, make phone calls, and get in touch with agencies and headhunters, but first—there was always a "first"—he had to run by the church to help repair the roof, or he had to mow his yard, or he had to go by the gym to work out his sore muscles, or he had to sit down and figure out a new budget . . .

Nick knew he couldn't keep putting off his job hunt. *Help me, God.* He picked up his organizer and started making notes.

᪥ Everyone has something in his life that he seems to put off doing. It may be finishing a college degree, buying a house, or applying for a promotion. It may be something simple like painting the house, cleaning the garage, or balancing the checkbook. Ultimately, if some project never gets accomplished you have no one to blame except yourself. What a waste to look back and say, "If only I had . . ." Make yourself accountable to God to get yourself moving.

᪥ TRY THIS: *Write down three things: (1) something fun you have always wanted to do; (2) some career related activity you have put off; and (3) some family issue you have avoided confronting. Start today to accomplish one of these three items. Set yourself a goal of one month to have all three completed. Keep a check on your progress each week.*

GO AHEAD AND BE LAZY; SLEEP ON, BUT YOU WILL GO HUNGRY.

PROVERBS 19:15 GNT

A FARMER TOO LAZY TO PLOW HIS FIELDS AT THE RIGHT TIME WILL HAVE NOTHING TO HARVEST.

PROVERBS 20:4 GNT

A lazy person, whatever the talents with which he set out, will have condemned himself to second-hand thoughts and to second-rate friends.

CYRIL CONNOLLY

Paying Attention

You may think that everything you do is right, but remember that the LORD judges your motives.

~ *Proverbs 21:2* GNT

A GOOD FRIEND CAN TELL YOU WHAT IS THE MATTER WITH YOU IN A MINUTE.
—ARTHUR BRISBANE

The small knot of men joked as they leaned on the fence and looked at the donkey, "That's you, Drew, with your feet dug in at the gate." The other men chuckled, but Drew asked George what he meant. "You have a habit of ignoring everything else that's going on around you, Drew," George explained. "You have one way of doing things, and that's your way."

"You know you're our pal, Drew," Keith chimed in. "But you do always seem to take over." At first, Drew stung from those words. Then he realized only true friends could be that direct and honest.

After thinking about his friends' words for a couple days, Drew realized they were speaking the truth. He did take over, often at the expense of others, he admitted to himself. Wanting to change and become more considerate, Drew went back to George and Keith to ask for help. Drew asked them to say the word *donkey* whenever they noticed that attitude again.

A donkey will become immovable when he makes up his mind about going or not going—regardless of what anyone says. When your mind is set on doing something your way, you miss seeing how it affects others. Maybe you have good intentions, but if you fail to consider the needs and feelings of others, you only alienate friends and thwart your efforts. Keeping your ears open and paying attention to what is happening around you will allow you to be more considerate of others.

Try this: Place a small picture of a donkey on your bathroom mirror. Each morning, think about yourself and ask God to keep you from digging in your heels and ignoring others. Share this story with a trusted friend and agree to help each other avoid such mistakes. Use the code word donkey when you see a lapse in judgment happening.

An honest answer is a sign of true friendship.

Proverbs 24:26
GNT

Pay attention and listen to the sayings of the wise.

Proverbs 22:17 NIV

When two people relate to each other authentically and humanly, God is the electricity that surges between them.

Martin Buber

THE SPIDER'S WEB

If you stay calm, you are wise, but if you have a hot temper, you only show how stupid you are.

~ *Proverbs 14:29* GNT

THERE IS NO GREAT ACHIEVEMENT THAT IS NOT THE RESULT OF PATIENT WORKING AND WAITING.
—JOSIAH HOLLAND

Aaron started to close the screen door. Just then he realized there was a large spider working on spinning a web across one corner of the doorframe. The spider worked meticulously to attach the web from one crosspiece to the next. Then Aaron watched as the spider let himself down a good distance. At first he just hung there, and then finally the spider began to sway. After several unsuccessful attempts, the spider finally attached his string farther out on the doorframe and quickly worked to connect the new layer to the rest of the web.

Aaron watched for quite some time. His first thought was that he would never have the patience to do something that intricate. He liked to do things quickly, to make decisions without hesitation, to take action without debate. The longer he watched, however, the more he understood what calm, persistent patience could really accomplish.

When spinning a web, a spider is focused on the task at hand. At times, he must make a number of attempts before a new string is connected. But always there is patience enough to accomplish the final goal. Like the spider, you should eagerly approach tasks with a high level of patience. Weigh the options, seek experienced counsel, and ensure you are following the wisest plan of action. You develop godly patience through prayers and consistent daily practice.

Try this: *Ask yourself these questions as you begin each new task: (1) What are the facts? (2) What are three possible ways to approach this? (3) Who has done something like this before? (4) How would Jesus respond if he were doing it? Demonstrate godly patience in your actions at home, in your community, and at work.*

Enthusiasm without knowledge is not good; impatience will get you into trouble.

Proverbs 19:2 GNT

Do you see a man who speaks in haste? There is more hope for a fool than for him.

Proverbs 29:20 NIV

Our patience will achieve more than our force.

Edmund Burke

All Creation Sings

I love to walk along the path
That leads around the hill;
At evening is the time to hear
The active whippoorwill.
I marvel at the handiwork
Of nature's wondrous plan,
And breathe the balmy evening air—
The nature God gave man.
Sometimes we don't appreciate
The beauty that we see,
But God's created handiwork
Was made for you and me.

William A. Bixler

There are four things that are too mysterious for me to understand: an eagle flying in the sky, a snake moving on a rock, a ship finding its way over the sea, and a man and a woman falling in love.

~ *Proverbs 30:18–19 GNT*

I LOOKED UPON THE WORKS OF GOD IN THIS VISIBLE CREATION . . . MY HEART WAS TENDER AND OFTEN CONTRITE, AND A UNIVERSAL LOVE TO MY FELLOW CREATURES WAS INCREASED IN ME.

JOHN WOOLMAN

The Seeds You Sow

A hard-working farmer has plenty to eat, but it is stupid to waste time on useless projects.

~ *Proverbs* 12:11 GNT

Derek and Jordan were neighbors who agreed to plant a small vegetable garden together. They would each help care for it and share the produce with their families. The friends looked forward to spending time together on the project, but neither realized how involved the task would become.

It took time digging up the soil and breaking up the hard clods. Planting the seeds required precision. Some had to be deeper than others; some were planted side by side; others were planted three inches apart; and still others were planted eight inches apart. As the seeds sprouted, a portion of the plants required stakes to support them. Watering, weeding, fertilizing, and cultivating took a lot of time, but the guys kept their end goal in mind.

Finally, they began to see the fruits of their labor—tomatoes, squash, beans, cucumbers, and other vegetables. As they harvested their crops Derek remarked, "Aren't you glad we don't do this for a living? It's fun, but it takes a lot of work."

The time and energy it takes to grow a vegetable garden can be compared to the effort it takes to "grow" your life. You must fill your life with healthy, nourishing influences. Be careful of what you read, what you listen to, whom you talk with, where you go, and whom you choose for friends. Living a life that is fulfilling requires planning ahead and maintaining your "soil" daily. The value of your life will be measured by the positive impact you have on yourself and others.

TRY THIS: *Plant something new today either outside or in your house. As you carefully tend it over the next weeks and months, compare it to your life. If your "soil" is dry or undernourished, grow your life through daily devotion and Bible reading. Surround yourself with a group of Christian friends to help you maintain your daily walk.*

HE WHO GATHERS IN SUMMER IS A SON WHO ACTS WISELY, BUT HE WHO SLEEPS IN HARVEST IS A SON WHO ACTS SHAMEFULLY.

PROVERBS 10:5 NASB

A HARD-WORKING FARMER HAS PLENTY TO EAT. PEOPLE WHO WASTE TIME WILL ALWAYS BE POOR.

PROVERBS 28:19 GNT

We plough the fields and scatter the good seed on the land, but it is fed and watered by God's Almighty hand.

JANE MONTGOMERY CAMPBELL

A Bright Future

Wisdom is good for the soul. Get wisdom and you have a bright future.

~ *Proverbs 24:14 GNT*

> KNOWLEDGE IS
> HORIZONTAL.
> WISDOM IS
> VERTICAL—IT
> COMES DOWN
> FROM ABOVE.
> —BILLY GRAHAM

Victor had been confident of his opinions ever since college, and he expected that his boys would grow up to view the world as he did. Now he wasn't so sure anymore. His twin sons, David and Danny, were popular, smart, and dedicated Christians. But the futures they planned after graduation were exactly opposite—David was joining the Army, and Danny, well, Danny was joining the Peace Corps.

How could his boys make such contrary choices? Even their haircuts were different. Victor didn't understand. "What do you think?" Victor asked his neighbor. His friend said that Victor seemed to be simultaneously trying to reconcile war with peace.

Victor prayed for understanding, and then it occurred to him. David and Danny both had a heart for Christ, and they both actually had the same goal—both of them wanted peace, and they were simply working toward the same goal in different ways. They both had a bright future. *Thank you, God, for giving me a glimpse of your wisdom.*

꧁ It's easy to consider only one or a few angles when pondering a problem. Sometimes you have to stretch your mind to consider all facets of a situation. And sometimes these "facets" may be a new wrinkle in your awareness. Mental habits can sometimes act as mental blinders. Seek God's wisdom by maintaining a constant relationship with him through reading the Bible daily and talking to him in prayer. The more you seek God's wisdom for each situation, the more you will attain it.

꧁ TRY THIS: *A good mental exercise for stretching your mind is to pick a word at random and see how many meanings you can think of. Try this with the word peace, for example. An unabridged dictionary is likely to list around fifteen different usages, but the point isn't to compete with a dictionary; the point is to st-r-e-t-ch your thinking.*

HAPPY IS ANYONE WHO BECOMES WISE—WHO COMES TO HAVE UNDERSTANDING.

PROVERBS 3:13 GNT

TO BE WISE YOU MUST FIRST HAVE REVERENCE FOR THE LORD. IF YOU KNOW THE HOLY ONE, YOU HAVE UNDERSTANDING.

PROVERBS 9:10 GNT

Of all human pursuits the pursuit of wisdom is the most perfect, the most sublime, the most profitable, the most delightful.

SAINT THOMAS AQUINAS

121

Rambling Roots

A man cannot be established through wickedness, but the righteous cannot be uprooted.

~ *Proverbs 12:3 NIV*

Alex and Judson were hiking through the Redwood Forest of Southern California. They marveled at the extreme height of the trees, the massive trunks of some, and the overall density. Coming across a park ranger, Judson asked, "For trees this huge, how deep are their roots?"

The park ranger explained that the redwoods actually have a shallow root system. Instead of growing deep, the roots spread out great distances right under the surface of the ground and intertwine with one another. Because the roots are wrapped together, the trees are able to grow taller and withstand the storms. The great strength of the forest comes from the roots of all the trees helping to support each other.

As they continued on their hike, Alex and Judson talked about how their lives were a lot like those trees. When they stood beside each other and helped each other, they always felt more strength and energy. The guys were glad they could count on each other for support.

In the same way as the roots of the trees, you need to know you can count on friends to be with you through the good times and the difficult times. The only way this can happen is by demonstrating that same commitment to your friends. But it takes more than just two trees (or friends) holding each other up. It's important to let God intertwine your lives. His strength will sustain you through any of life's storms, and he will help friends grow closer together.

Try this: Jot down the names of four friends. Beside each name, list something you can do this week to demonstrate your friendship and support: begin a workout routine together, write a card of encouragement and mail it, or help him with a painting project at his house. Look for ways to exhibit godly support to your friends.

Jonathan said to David, "Go in peace, for we have sworn friendship with each other in the name of the Lord."

I Samuel 20:42 NIV

Dear friends, let us love one another, because love comes from God.

I John 4:7 GNT

To have a good friend is one of the highest delights of life.

Author Unknown

God's Paint Set

Listen, my child, be wise and give serious thought to the way you live.

~ *Proverbs 23:19 GNT*

Be thou my vision, O Lord of my heart.
—Mary Elizabeth Byrne

The family drove across the flat desert of Arizona as the sun moved below the horizon. The sky became more vibrant with each passing moment. Tanner said, "Dad, look! God spilled his paint set!" It was beautiful. Just like a watercolor portrait.

Then Tanner asked: "Dad, how does the sun know which way to go every day?" His father explained that God has a plan for everything. God put the sun in the sky and the earth rotates around it. We see it rise in the east and set in the west.

Tanner continued: "But does God tell people where to go, too?" Dad shared that God also had a perfect plan for each person. Yet, unlike the sun, God lets people make choices. Just like there are many different roads to drive on, there are many ways to do things. We make the right choices by listening to God. Tanner said, "I'd rather God paint me a picture to follow."

The path you travel is your choice. If ever in doubt as to where you should go or what you should do, ask God to direct you. God is always with you. His desire is for you to make the right choices, and yet his love allows you to make your own choices. Before choosing one path over another, spend some time reading God's Word and praying for God to reveal his will for your life. Open your mind to God, and receive insight and assurance.

TRY THIS: *Go outside and watch the sunset today. Spend a few minutes in the fading light and thank God for all he's done for you. When the light is gone, pause to praise God. Ask him to guide you tomorrow in everything you do, from sunrise to sunset.*

WISE PEOPLE WALK THE ROAD THAT LEADS UPWARD TO LIFE, NOT THE ROAD THAT LEADS DOWNWARD TO DEATH.

PROVERBS 15:24 GNT

THE WAY OF THE LAZY IS OVERGROWN WITH THORNS, BUT THE PATH OF THE UPRIGHT IS A LEVEL HIGHWAY.

PROVERBS 15:19 NRSV

Lift up thine eyes, and seek His Face. . . . Christ is the path, and Christ the prize.

JOHN SAMUEL BEWLEY MONSELL

Other books in the Proverbs for Life™ series:

Proverbs for Life™ for You
Proverbs for Life™ for Teens
Proverbs for Life™ for Women

All available from your favorite bookstore.
We would like to hear from you.
Please send your comments about this book to:

Inspirio™, the gift group of Zondervan
Attn: Product Development
Grand Rapids, Michigan 49530

www.inspirio.com

<u>Our mission:</u>
To provide distinctively Christian gifts that point people to God's Word
through refreshing messages and innovative designs.

inspirio™

The gift group of Zondervan